Pearson Baccalaureate

City Cat

Tony Langham
Illustrated by Lynne Willey

Chapter 1

Tabitha was a travelling cat. She was always on the move. She was always looking for new places to go and new people to see.

One day Tabitha got on a plane without anyone seeing her and went all the way to America.

The first thing Tabitha saw when she got to America was a big sign.
It said, 'Welcome to New York'.
Tabitha wondered what to do first.
There was so much to see in New York.
Off she went to look around.

New York was a very big city. It had lots of tall buildings – very tall buildings, and the streets were full of people, cars, buses and taxis. It was very noisy! Tabitha didn't know which way to go.

Then Tabitha saw some people going down an escalator. She decided to follow them. Down, down, down she went.

At the bottom of the escalator was a platform and a long dark tunnel. Lots of people were waiting on the platform. Tabitha liked it down there because it was nice and quiet.
She lay down under a seat and went to sleep.

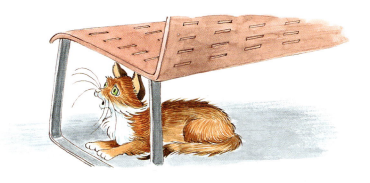

Suddenly Tabitha woke up with a jump. There was a very loud noise and something was coming out of the tunnel. Tabitha was very scared. She didn't wait to see what was making the noise. She just ran as fast as she could back along the tunnel and up the escalator. Up, up, up she went.

Without stopping to look, Tabitha ran out on to the street.

SCREEEEECH! A big yellow taxi nearly ran over her.

'You stupid cat!' the driver shouted.

Tabitha went on running until she got to the other side of the street. There she saw a sign to a park.

It was much quieter in the park and
there was lots of green grass and lots
of flowers. Tabitha sat on a wall and
watched all the people go by.
There were people running,
people riding bicycles,
people playing music
and even people juggling.
Some people were sitting on the grass
and eating sandwiches. Suddenly
Tabitha felt very hungry.

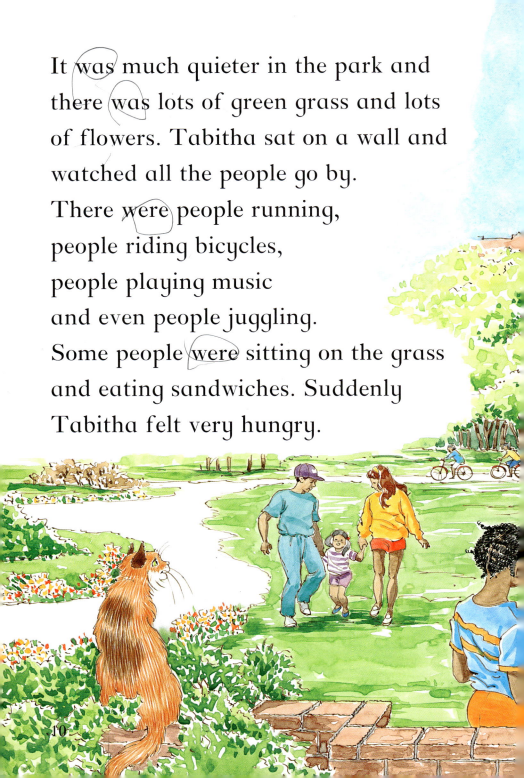

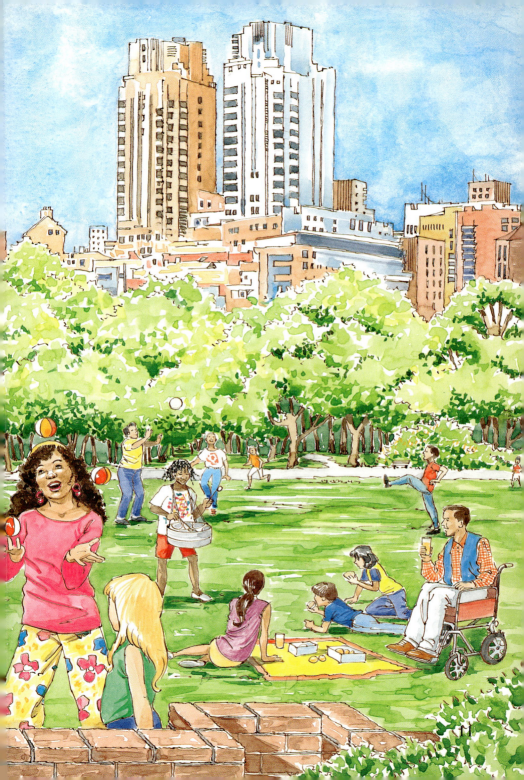

Just then Tabitha saw a little girl.
She was sitting on a bench next to
her mother, and she had a rag doll.
The girl was eating a big sandwich.
Tabitha hoped the girl might give her
some of the sandwich.

So Tabitha went over and sat down near the little girl. She looked up at her with hungry eyes. The little girl looked at Tabitha.

'Hello pussycat,' she said.

'Meow,' went Tabitha.

The little girl laughed.

'Did you hear that, Mum?' she said.

'This pussycat just said "hello".'

'That's nice, Helen,' said her mother, but she didn't look up from her book.

Helen looked at Tabitha.

'Do you want some of my sandwich?' she asked.

'Meow,' went Tabitha.

Helen threw Tabitha a bit of her sandwich and Tabitha ate it up very quickly. So Helen gave Tabitha some more bits and Tabitha ate up all those too. Soon all the sandwich was gone.

Just then Helen's mother said,
'Come on, Helen. It's time to go home.'
'Do we have to?' said Helen.
But her mother was already walking
off so Helen had to follow her.
Tabitha was sad to see them go.
She liked the little girl.
But then she saw the rag doll. Helen
had left it on the bench. Tabitha
jumped up, picked up the doll in her
mouth and ran off after the little girl.

Chapter 2

When Tabitha got to the park gates, she saw Helen and her mother getting on to a bus. She quickly ran after them. She jumped on to a car and then on to the roof of the bus. It started to move off down the street.

Tabitha liked riding on the roof of the bus. It was a much nicer way to see New York.

Inside the bus Helen suddenly said,
'Oh no! I've left my rag doll in the
park,' and she started to cry.
'Don't worry,' said her mother, 'we can
get you another one.'
But that didn't make Helen feel
any better.

Soon the bus stopped and Helen and her mother got off and walked down the street. Tabitha jumped down from the roof of the bus and ran after them. She saw them climb up some steps and go into a tall house. Tabitha stopped. She wondered how she could get into the house.

Tabitha walked to the end of the street and went round the backs of the houses. She found Helen's house and climbed up the fire escape.

She looked in the first window. Helen was not there.

Then she looked in the next window. There was Helen.

Helen was sitting on her bed. She looked very sad.

'Meow,' went Tabitha as loudly as she could.

Helen turned round. She couldn't believe her eyes. She opened the window and Tabitha jumped down on to the bed and gave Helen the rag doll.

'Oh thank you,' said Helen. 'What a clever pussycat you are!'

Just then Helen's mother came into the room. She saw Helen holding the rag doll.

'How did you get your rag doll back?' she asked Helen.

'The pussycat from the park followed us home. She gave it to me.'

'What cat?' asked Helen's mother.

'That one,' said Helen.
But when she turned round, Tabitha was not there.

Tabitha was already back in the street riding on the roof of a taxi - a big yellow New York taxi. She was off on her travels again. She never stayed in one place for long because Tabitha was a travelling cat.